This book belongs to

Name

Age

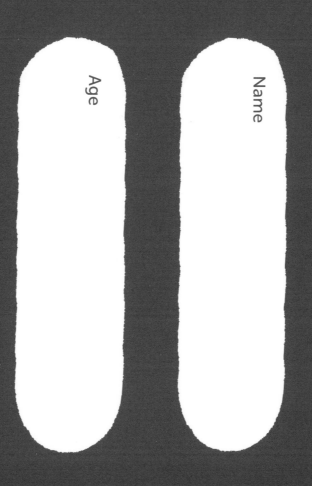

Save this book and all your amazing artwork
until you're all grown up!

ぬって Nutte © La Zoo 2010

First published in Japan in 2010 by Gakken Education Publishing Co., Ltd., Tokyo
Published in English by Downtown Bookworks Inc. by arrangement with Gakken Plus Co., Ltd.
English edition copyright Downtown Bookworks Inc. © 2017

Created and illustrated by La Zoo
Translated from the Japanese edition by Noriko Yoshimura

downtown bookworks

Downtown Bookworks Inc.
New York, New York
www.downtownbookworks.com
Printed in China
December 2020
978-1941367483
10 9 8 7 6 5 4 3 2

If you can hold a crayon or a pencil, you can make beautiful art!

● This book includes "starter art"—the beginnings of pictures that you will complete with crayons, colored pencils, or markers. Start on any page you like. You do not need to go from beginning to end in this book.

▶ Use whatever colors you like. And it is totally fine to color outside the lines.

◢◣ The most important thing is to have fun! You can follow the suggestions for what to draw on each page— or color anything else you want! YOU are the artist!

■ Be sure to share your work. And, if you are able to write your name, sign each creation.

On this page, you might want to add red strawberries or colored sprinkles to the ice cream cones. Draw eyes and a long tongue to make an ice cream monster!

Draw your favorite ice cream flavors.

Imagine you're eating an ice cream cone while you color this page.

Here, you will color the fireworks.

Kaboom! Fill the sky with fireworks!

On this page, you can tell a story and make art. The babies are crying. Maybe the babies are crying so much that their tears form an ocean with fish!

The babies are crying. Can you draw lots of tears?

Can you draw some baby toys to make them feel better?

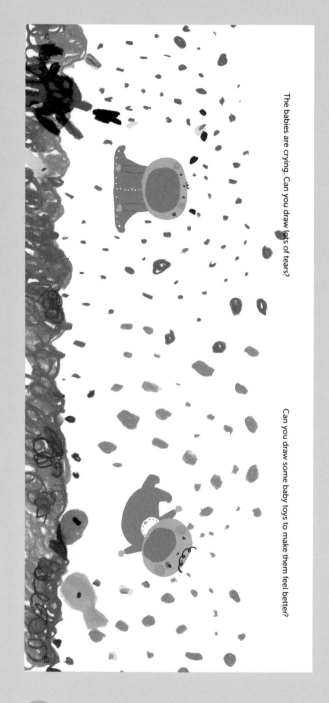

Every time you color and draw, you are telling a story.

When you make art, focus on expressing your imagination.
If you can't figure out what to draw, try to finish these sentences:
"It would be cool if there was a . . . " or "It would be fun if I could . . . "
And then have fun drawing what you dream up.

Draw whatever you imagine.

Do you want to draw a road? Maybe there are flowers along the road.
And buildings. And cars traveling on it....

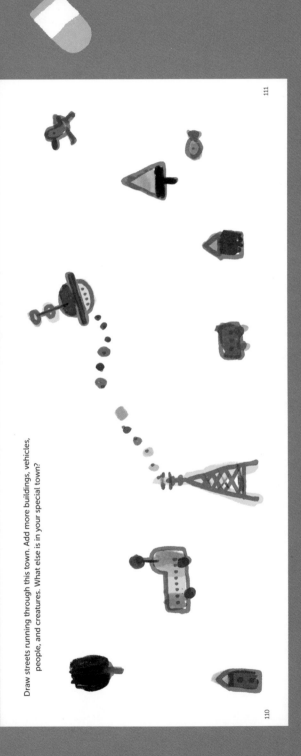

Draw streets running through this town. Add more buildings, vehicles,
people, and creatures. What else is in your special town?

111

110

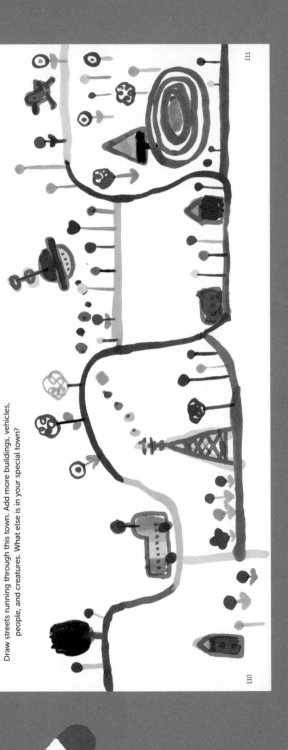

Draw streets running through this town. Add more buildings, vehicles,
people, and creatures. What else is in your special town?

111

110

Or maybe you
just want to fill
the page with
lots of cars...

Draw streets running through this town. Add more buildings, vehicles,
people, and creatures. What else is in your special town?

110

111

...or people,
and aliens—
and an elephant!

Draw streets running through this town. Add more buildings, vehicles,
people, and creatures. What else is in your special town?

110

111

Start drawing, and see where your imagination leads you. You'll have
lots of great ideas—and so much fun turning those ideas into art!

7

What color is this apple?

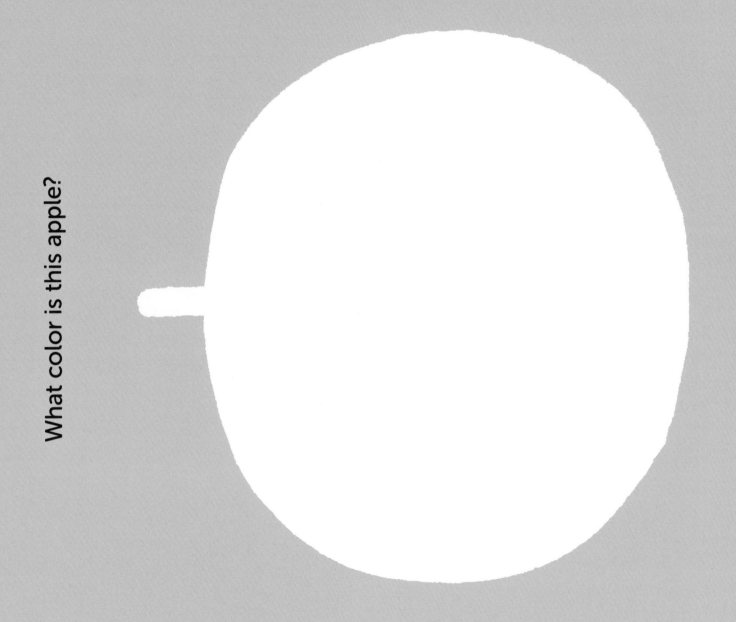

Color the bananas.

Fill in these balloons with your favorite colors and patterns.

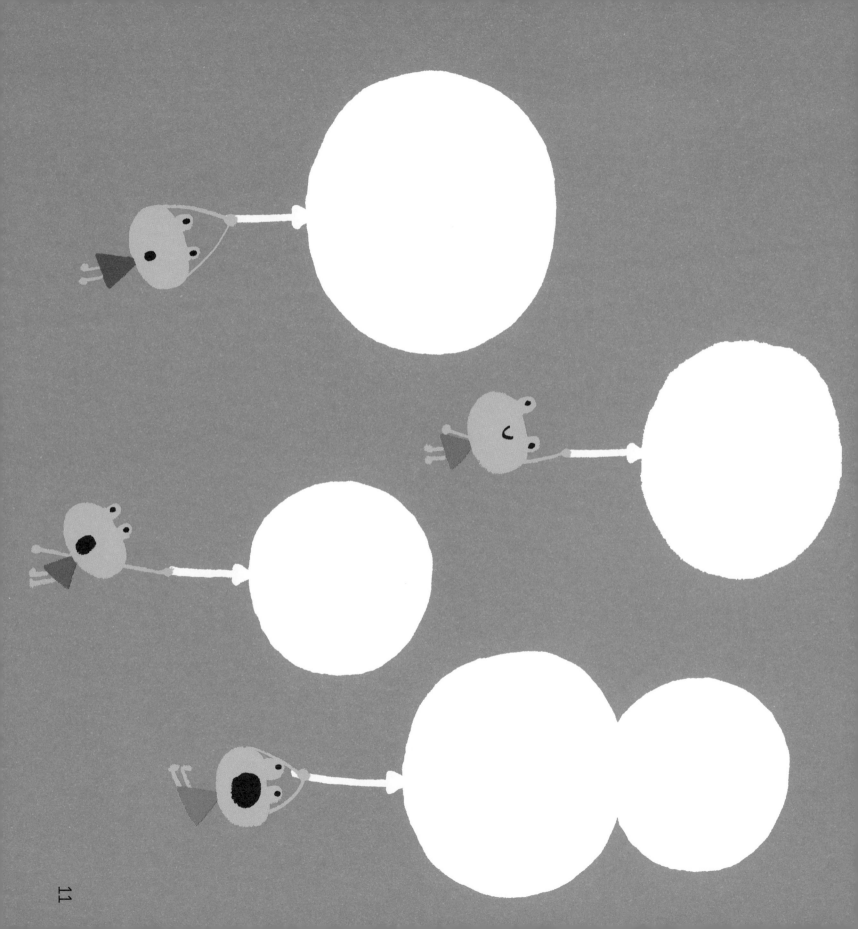

Make the fireflies glow.

Color the pineapple. Draw some more fruit!

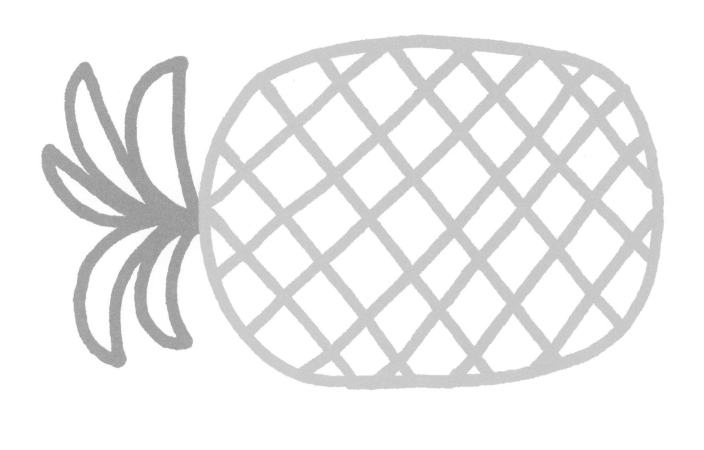

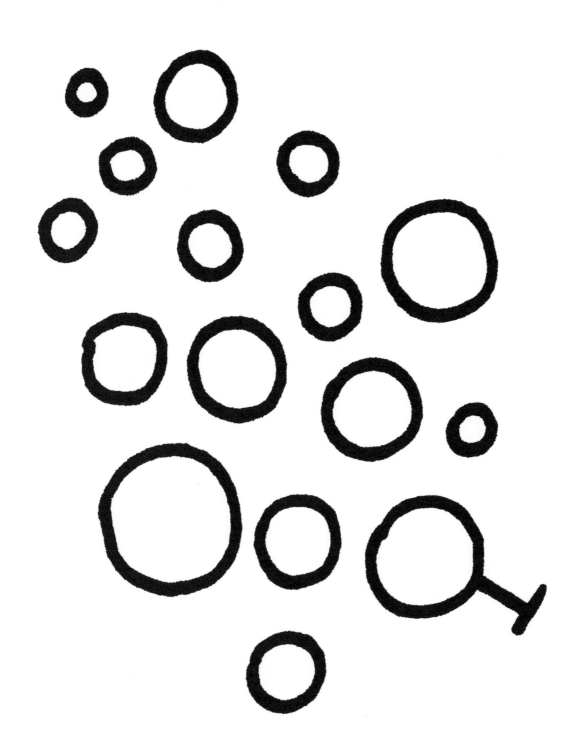

Color the grapes. Draw even more grapes to fill out the bunch.

Decorate these dinosaurs with any pattern you like.

Give these birds some beautiful feathers.

Design colorful sails for the sailboats.

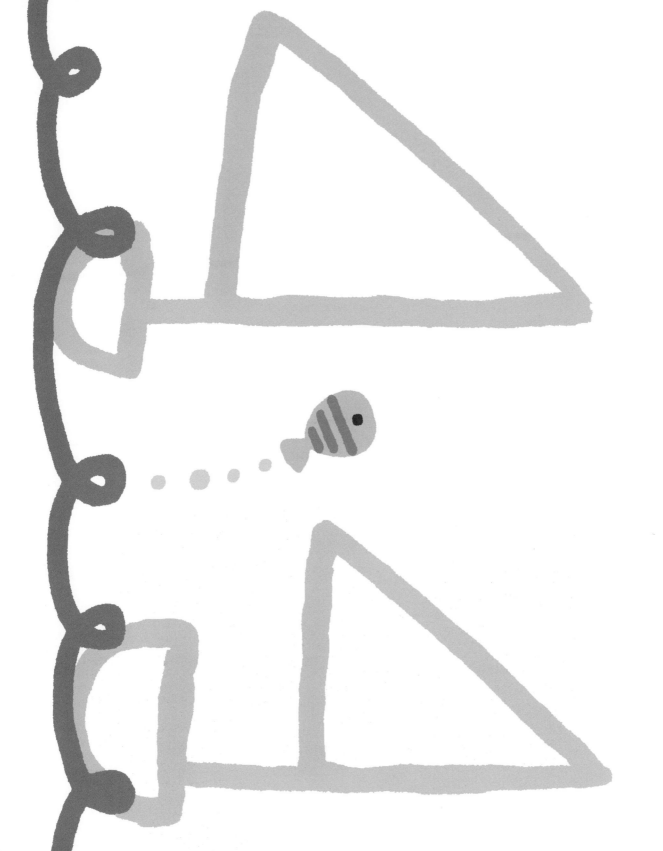

These dragons breathe fire. Can you draw the flames?

23

Decorate the cookies and candies.

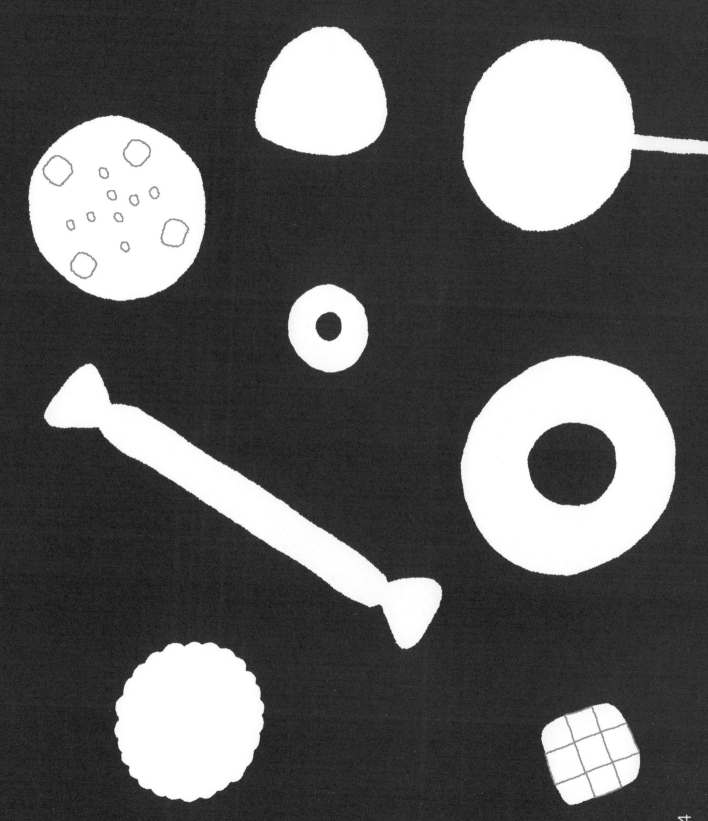

Color the window panes.

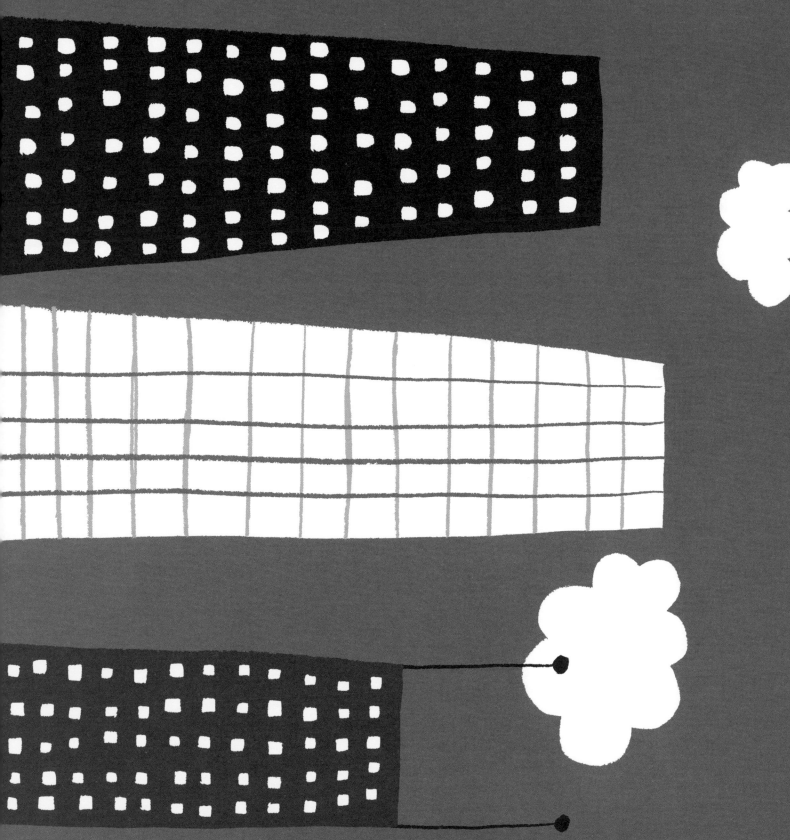

27

Are the ghosts scary or happy or sad? Color them in.
Draw some more friends for them.

Invent a pattern for the zebra.

Give this big cat some spots, stripes, or another pattern.

Can you give this boy a bow tie and some freckles?
Do you think he needs more hair?

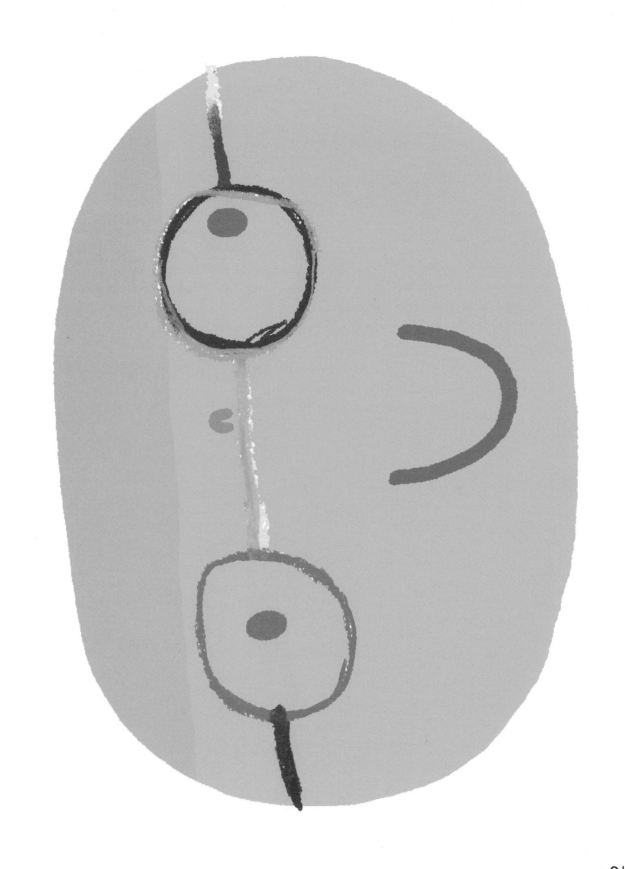

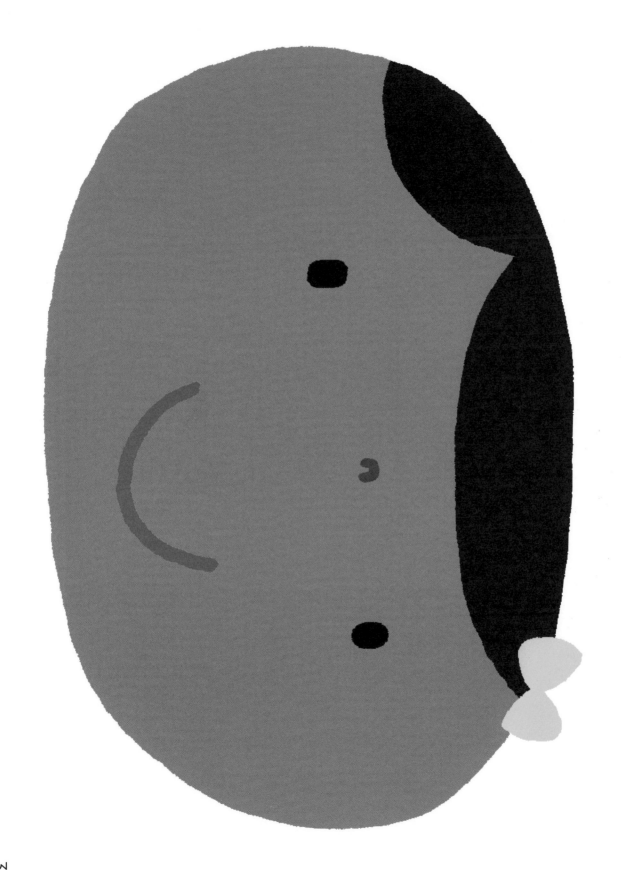

This girl needs glasses!

It's so sunny out! Can you give the lion some sunglasses? And a scarf?

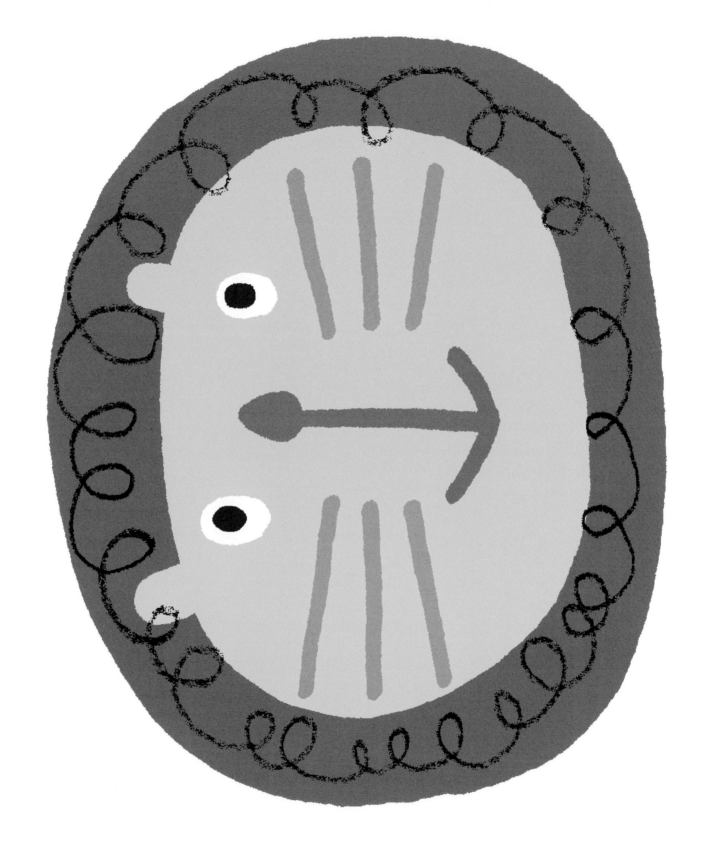

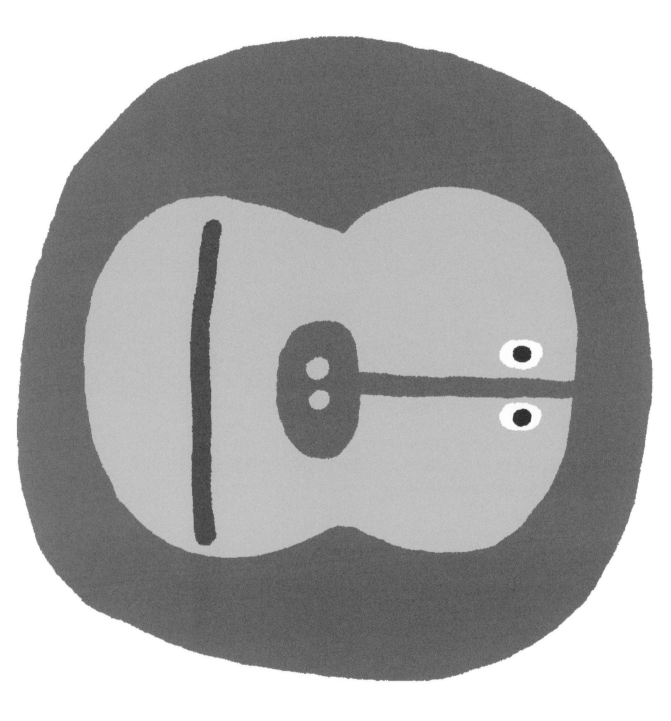

The monkey would like some glasses so he can see his lunch.
Can you draw his lunch too?

Have you ever seen a frog wearing glasses? Can you draw his books too? (He likes to read.)

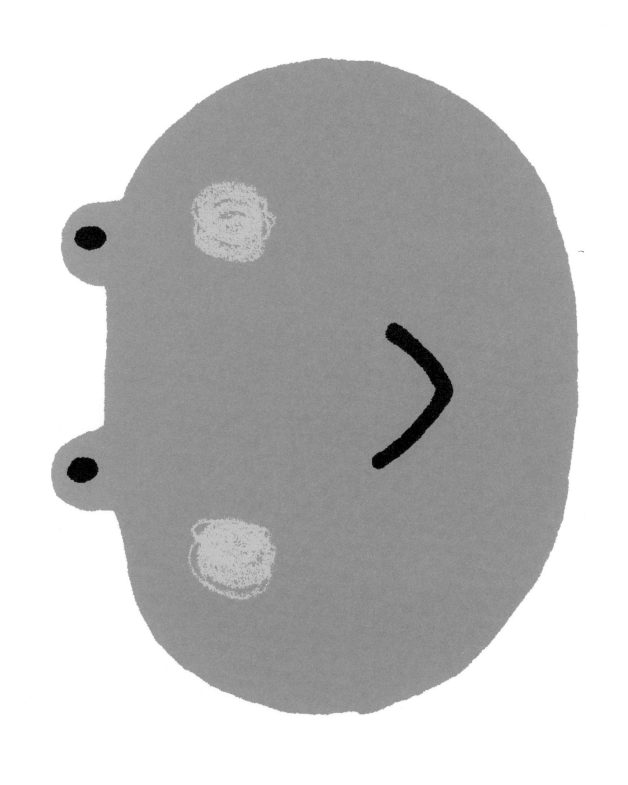

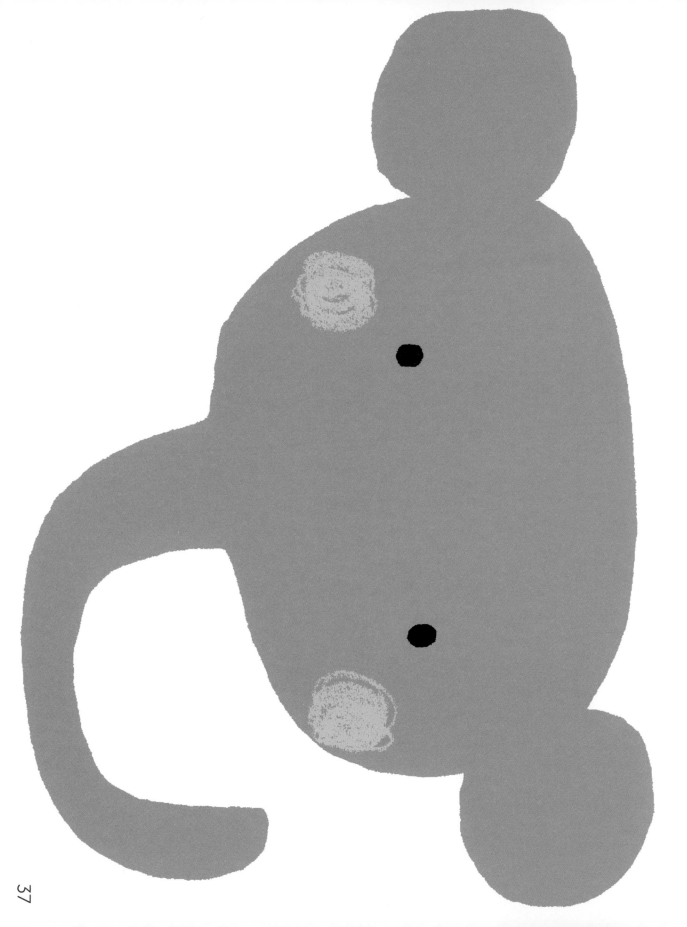

The elephant needs glasses to see his tiny friends.
Can you draw his glasses and his friends?

Clouds come in millions of different shapes and sizes. Draw some here.

Are there birds in the sky? Fish in the sea?

What's for dinner? Draw some food on the plate.

Everyone is blowing bubbles!
Draw bubbles all over the page.

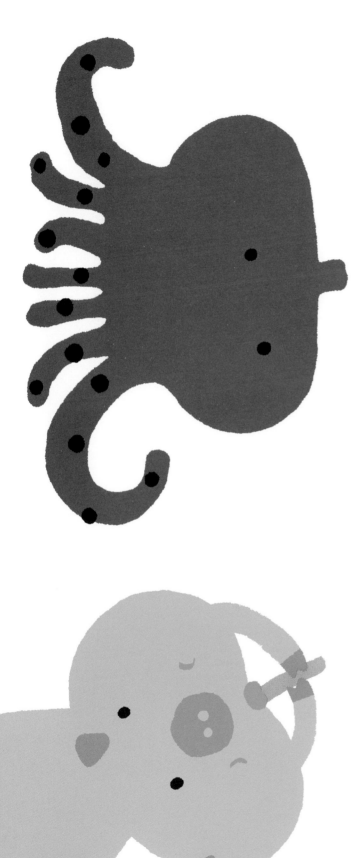

43

Elephants blow REALLY BIG bubbles.

OOPS! Spilled paint. Footprints everywhere. Draw more.

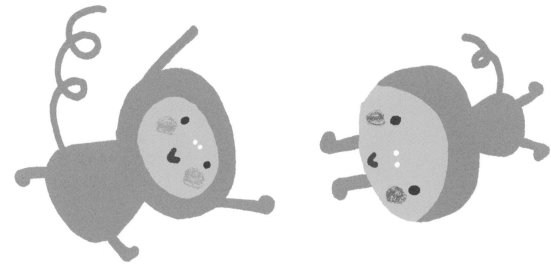

Color the beautiful garden.

48

49

Draw patterns on the fish.

These kids want curly hair.

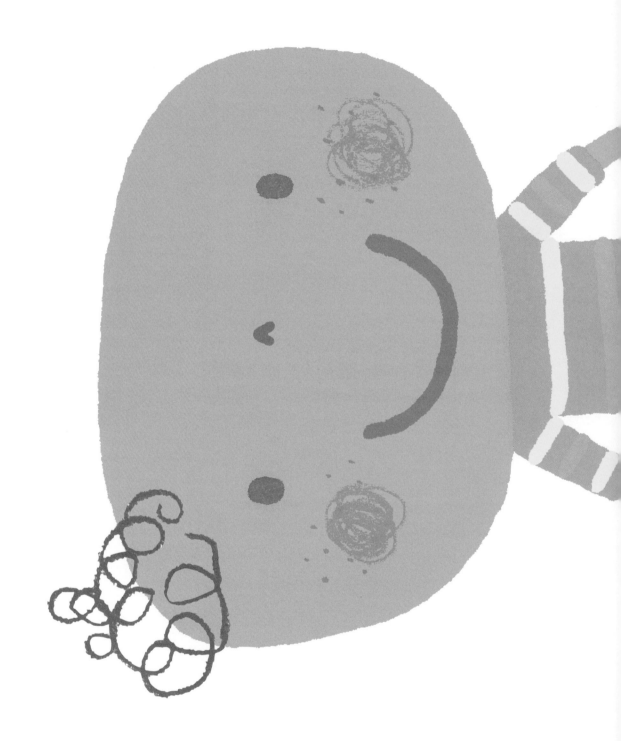

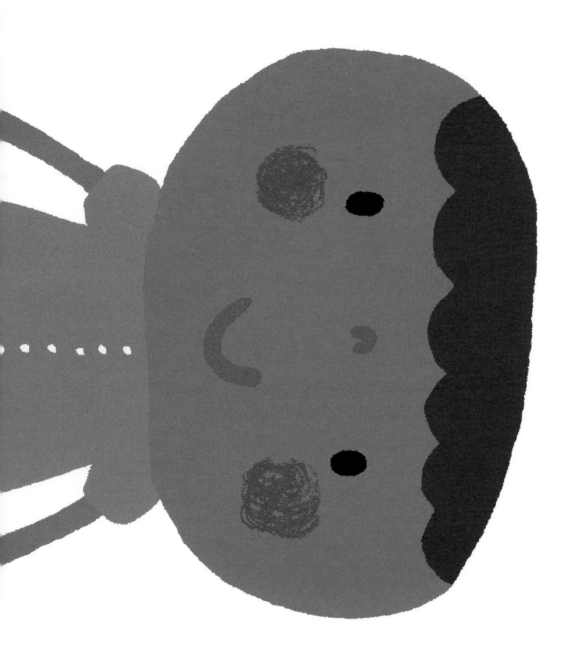

The pig and the monkey need tails.

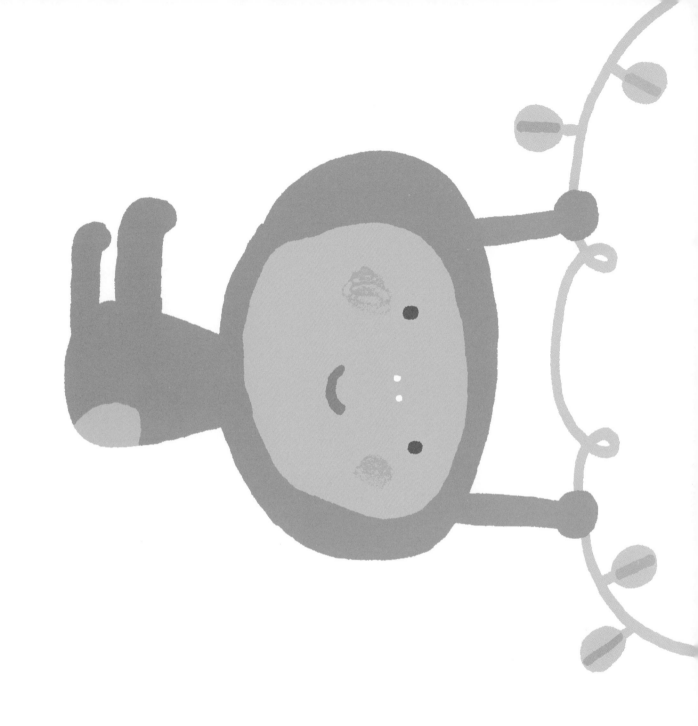

These animals are working up a real SWEAT!
Can you show the sweat dripping, flying, and spraying off their bodies? Draw some more runners too.

Someone got ahold of some lipstick and a jewelry box.
Can you draw more makeup and jewels on everybody?

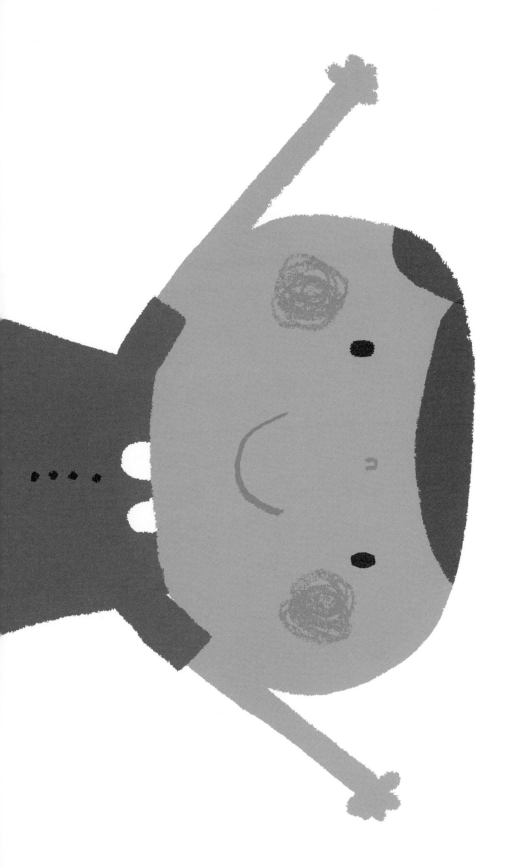

Everyone wants to play dress up!
Give them makeup, jewels, hats,
crowns, or whatever else you like!

The babies are crying. Can you draw lots of tears?

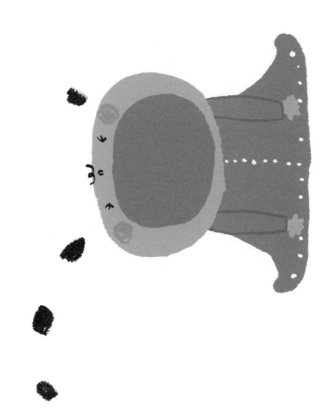

Can you draw some baby toys to make them feel better?

Give the sheep lots of fluffy wool.

Each of the penguin's hats should have a different color or pattern.

These hedgehogs aren't very scary without their quills.
Can you cover them with spiky quills?

Do you like to play in puddles? Cover this page with mud!

Color the children too.

Kaboom! Fill the sky with fireworks!

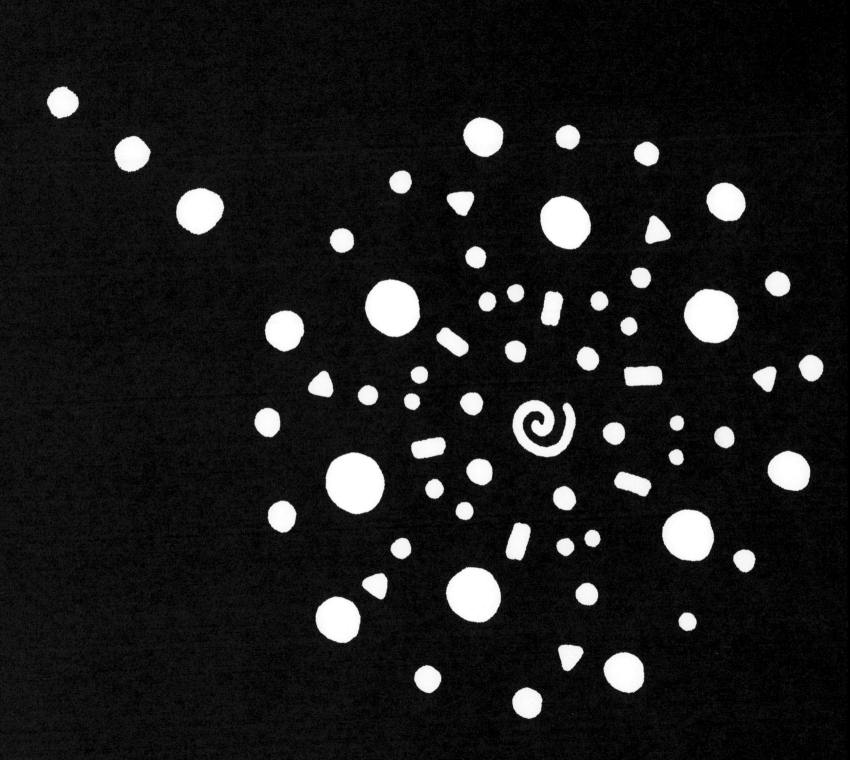

Create different patterns for these animals.

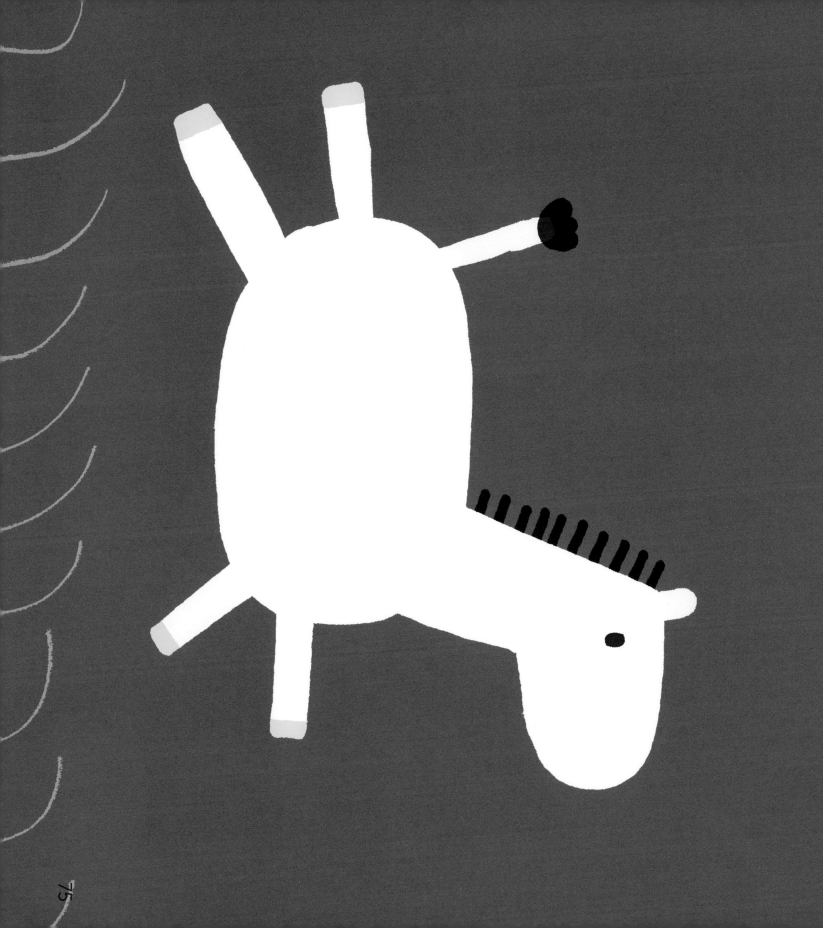

Imagine that it's cold and snowy. What do you see?
Create a winter wonderland.

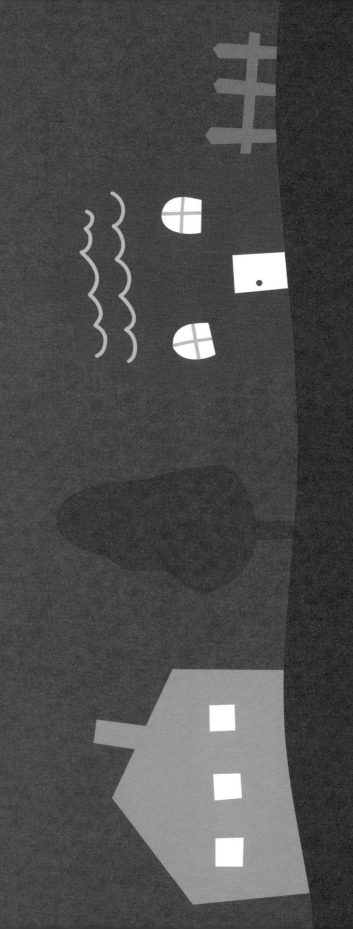

Can you draw some beards, mustaches, eyebrows, and sideburns on these guys?

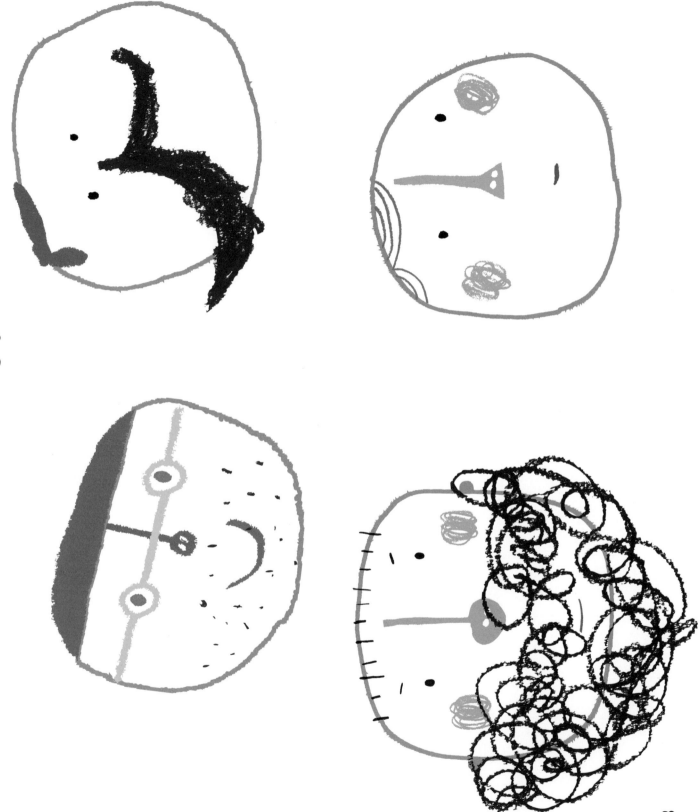

Do these kids have beards too? Crazy eyebrows?

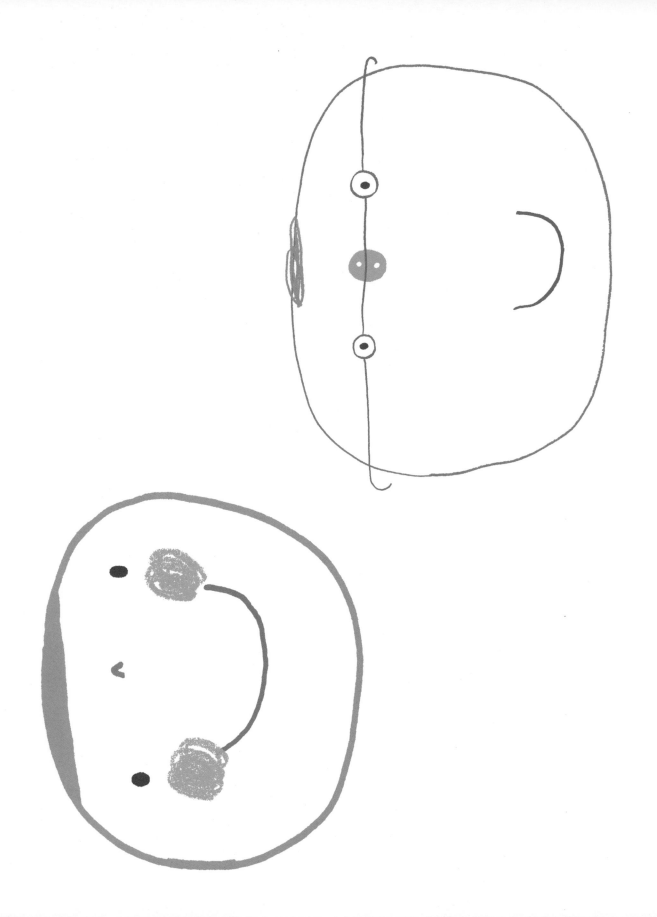

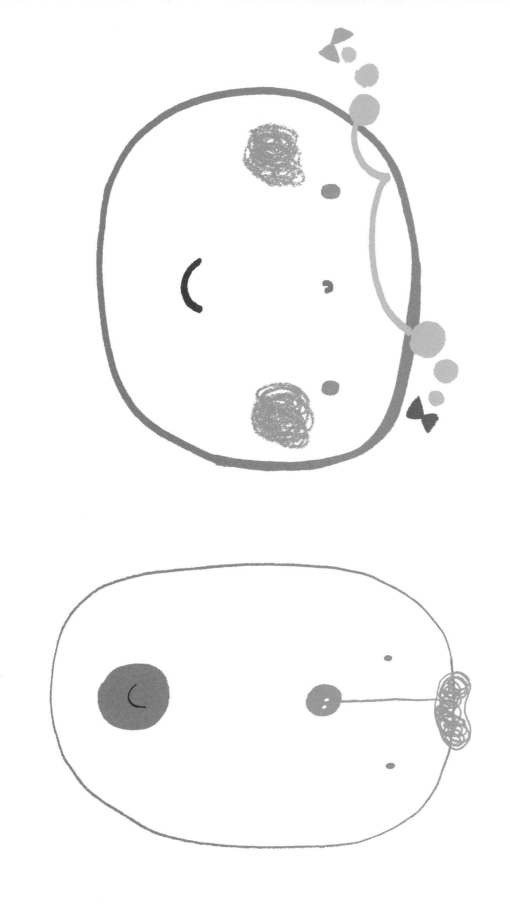

Give them some more hair, hats, bows, and whatever else you think they need.

Do robots and aliens have mustaches? Beards? Eyebrows?
What do they have on their faces?

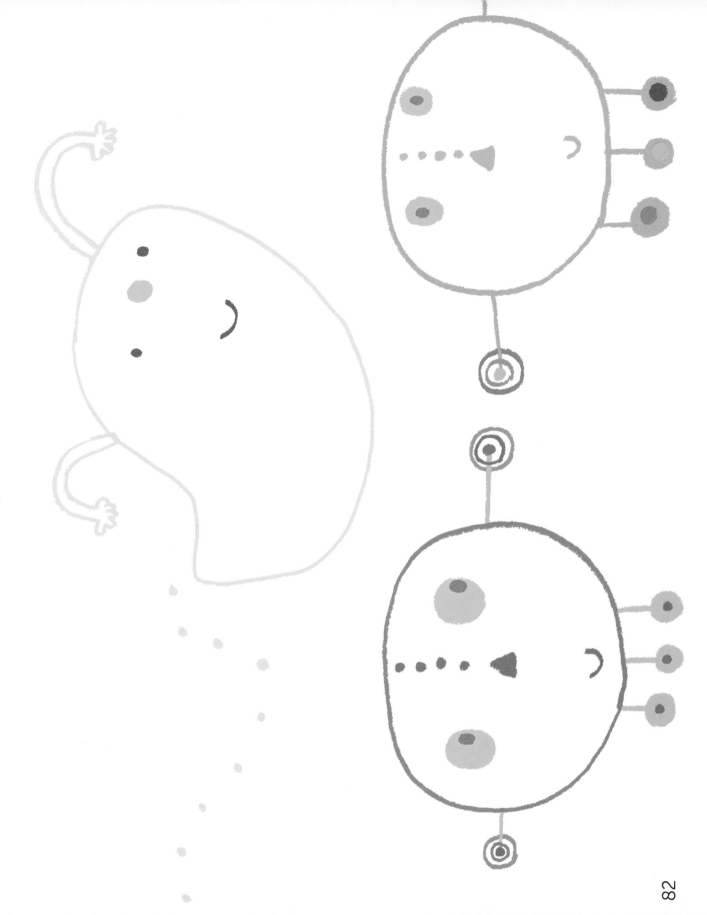

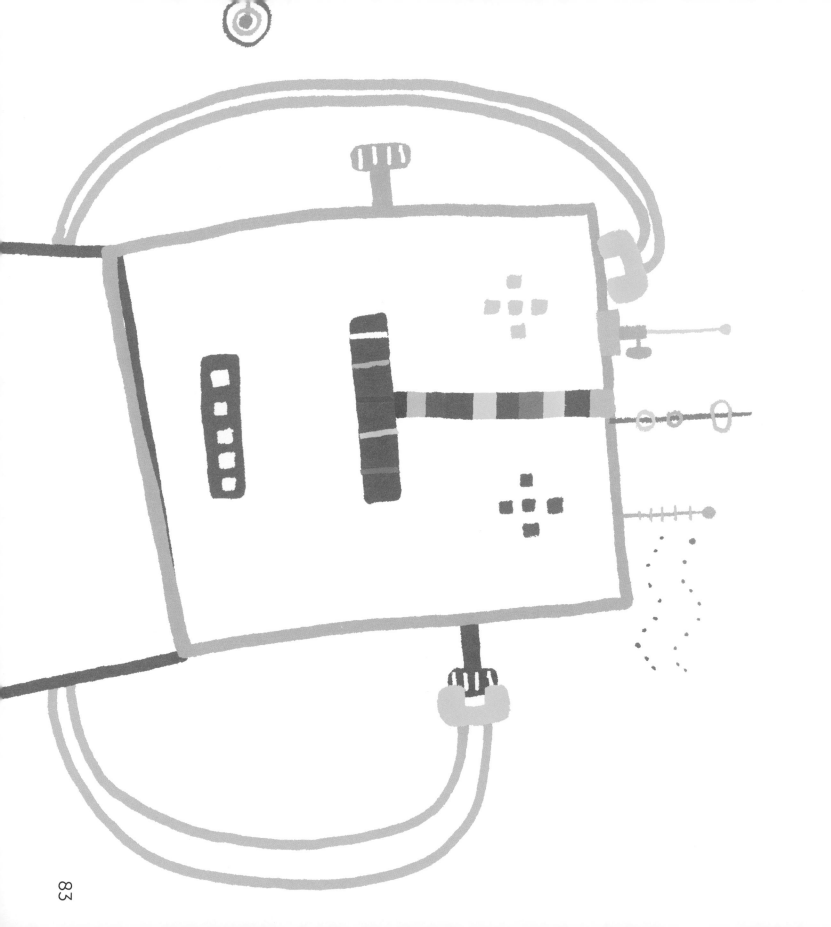

What is coming out of the smokestacks on these boats?

Turn each circle into something else.

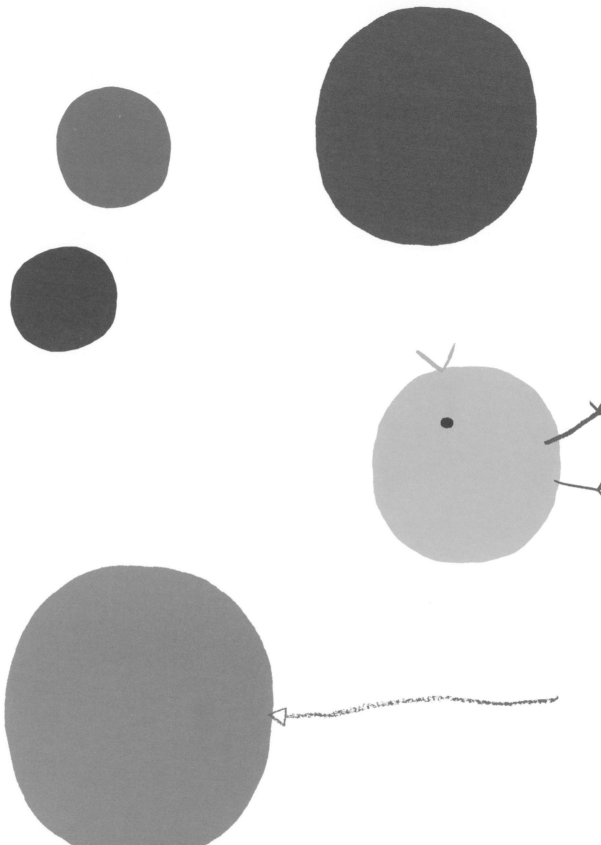

Here comes a giant whale. Draw water coming out of its spout.

And here's a little whale. Who is swimming with them?
Can you draw some more fish?

Draw your favorite ice cream flavors.

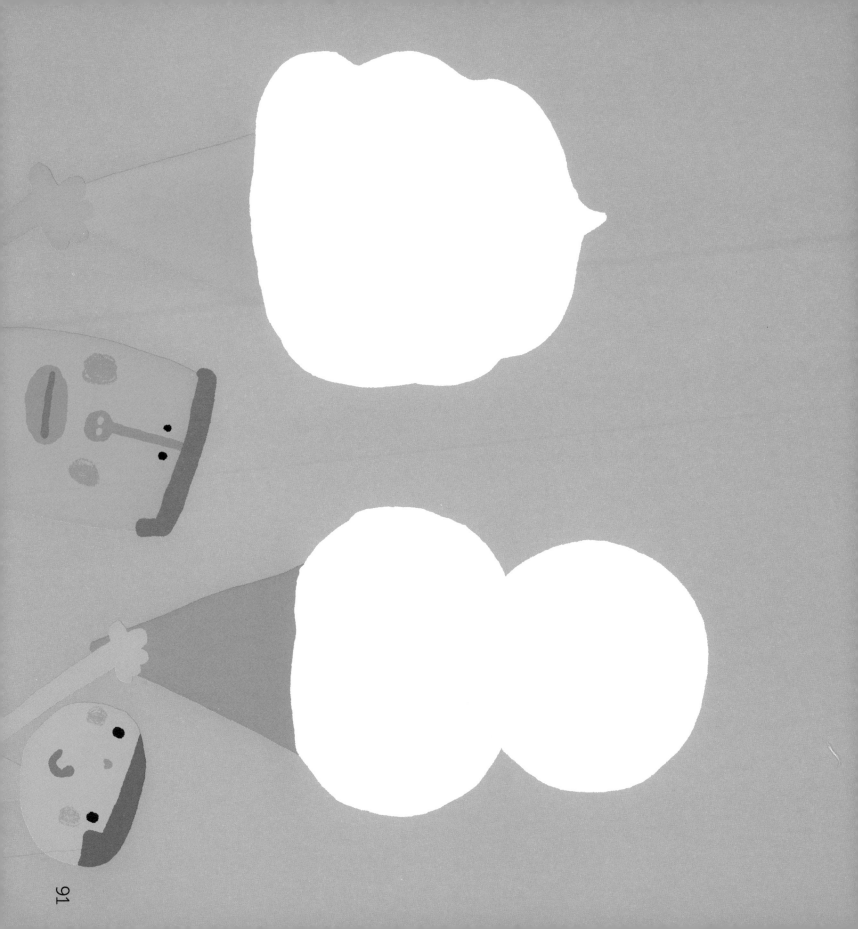

Help the elephant spray water at the octopus.

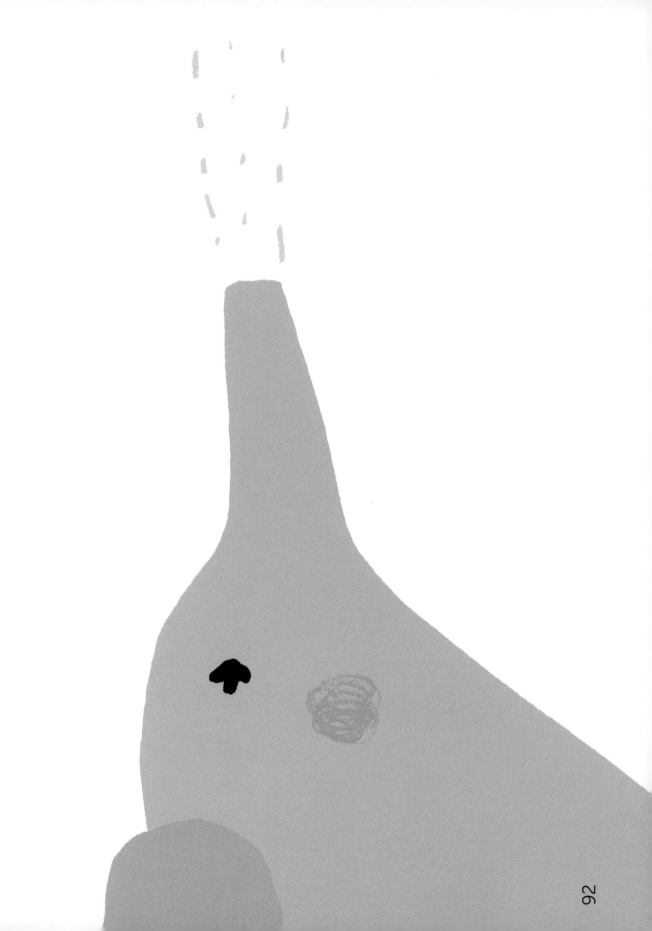

Help the octopus spray ink at the elephant.

The lion is washing his mane.

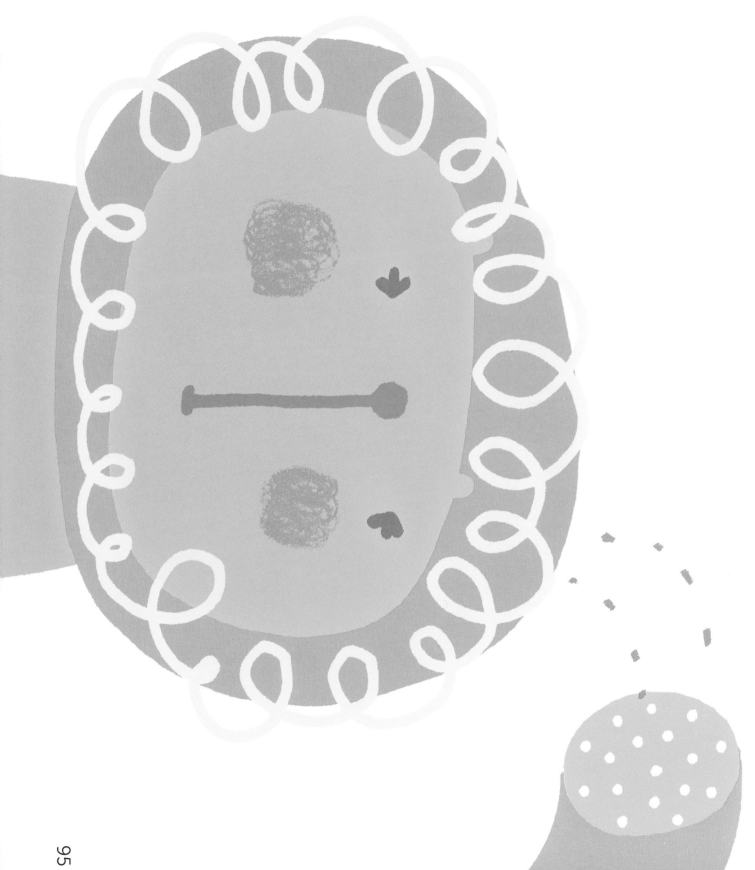

Rinse off the bubbles with lots of water!

It's raining! Draw the raindrops.

96

Color the airplane.

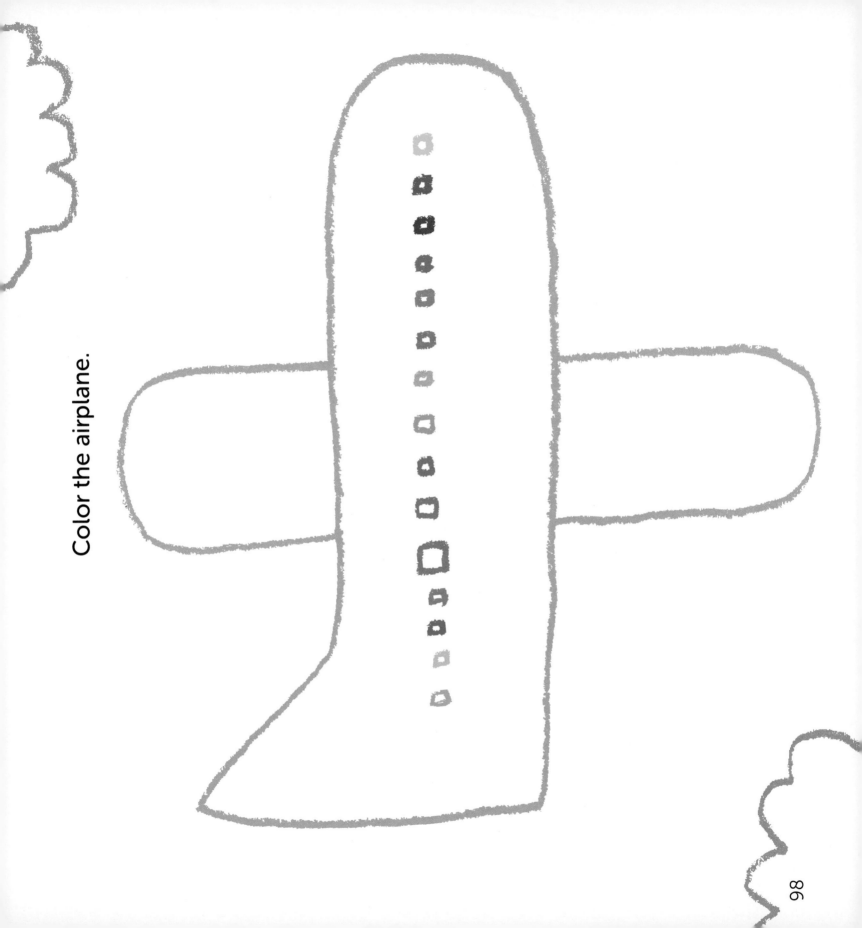

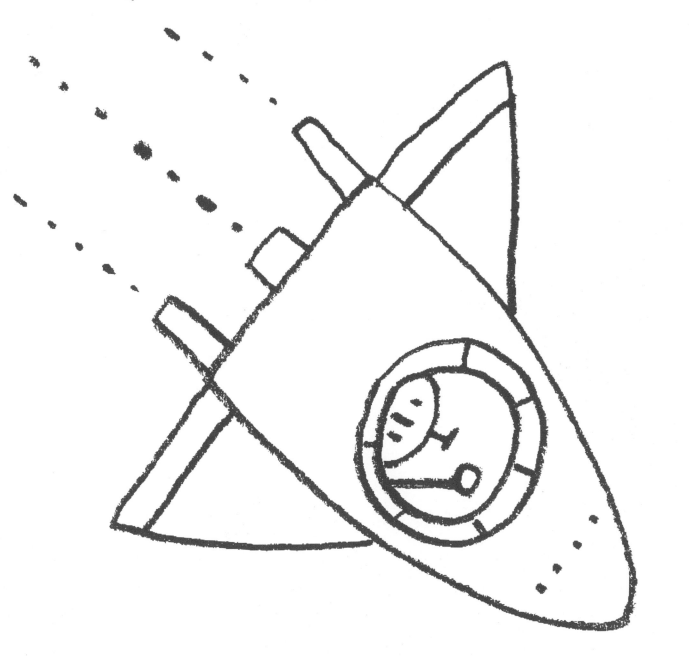

Color the rocket.

Draw different colors and patterns on the fingernails.

It's raining, it's pouring! Draw lots of raindrops.
Frogs love to get wet.

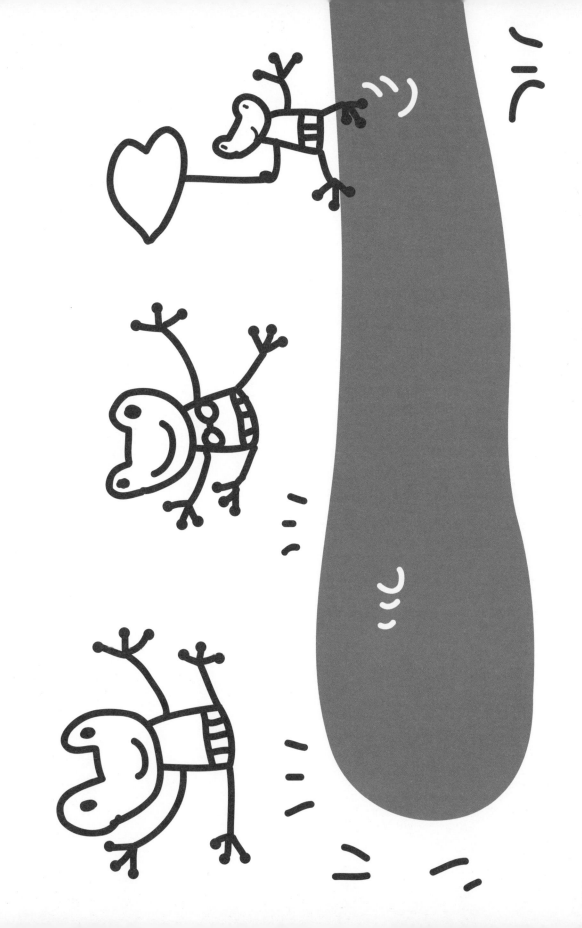

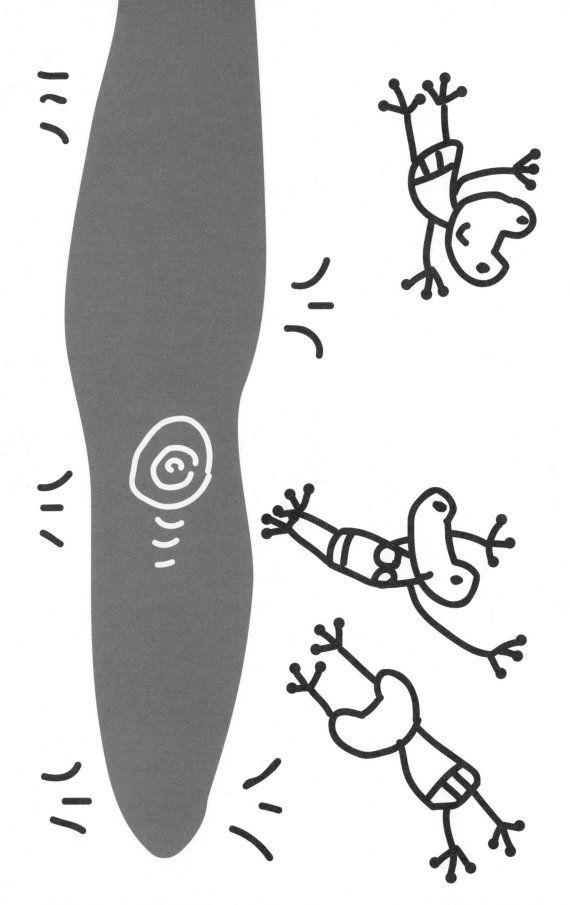

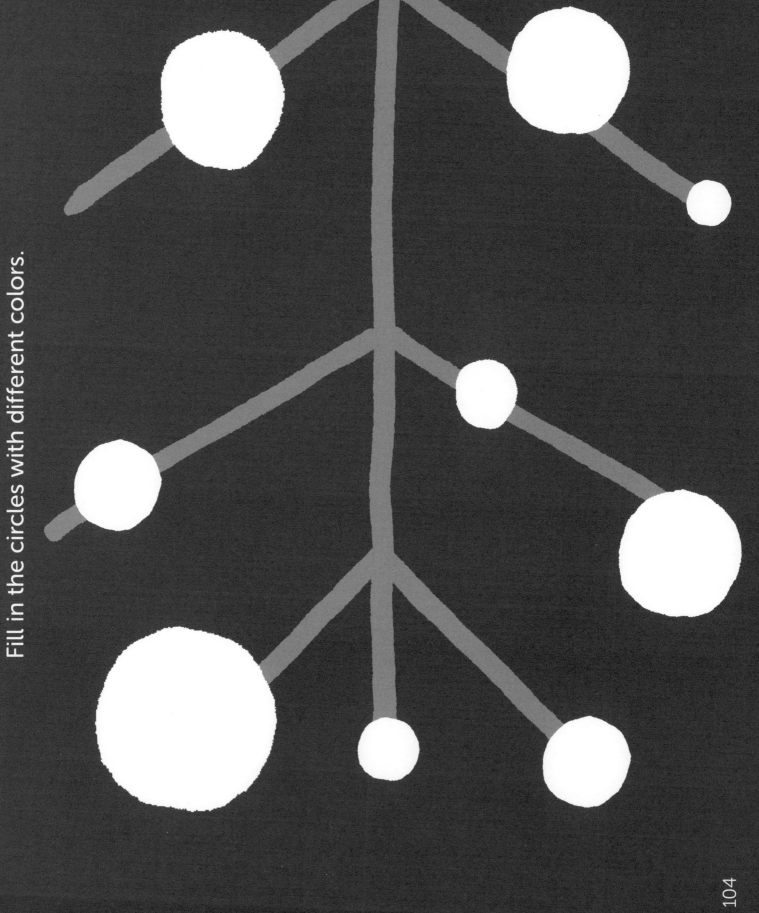

Fill in the circles with different colors.

Draw faces on the snowmen.

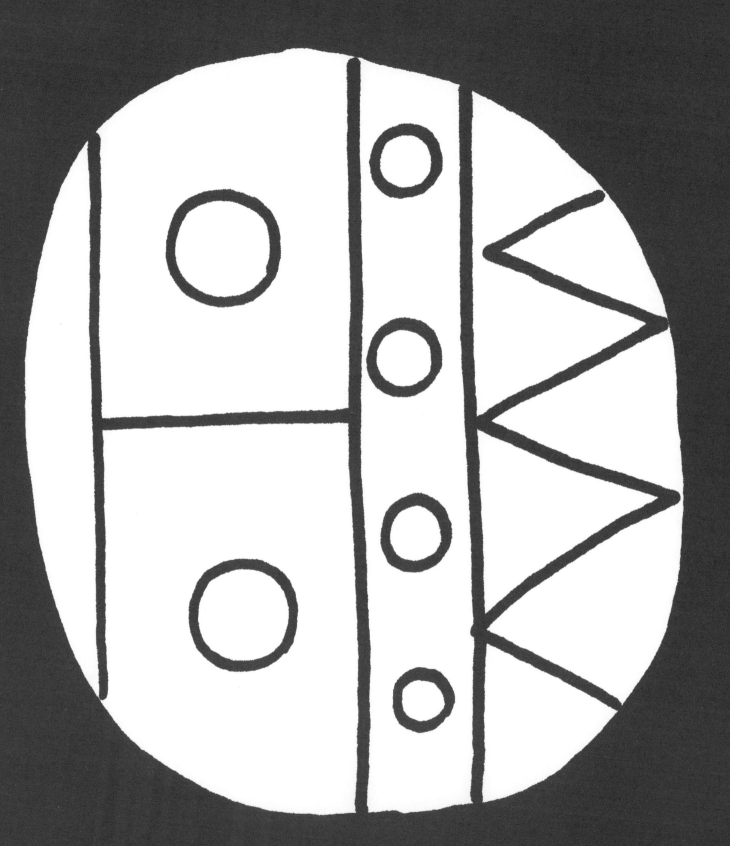

Make colorful masks.

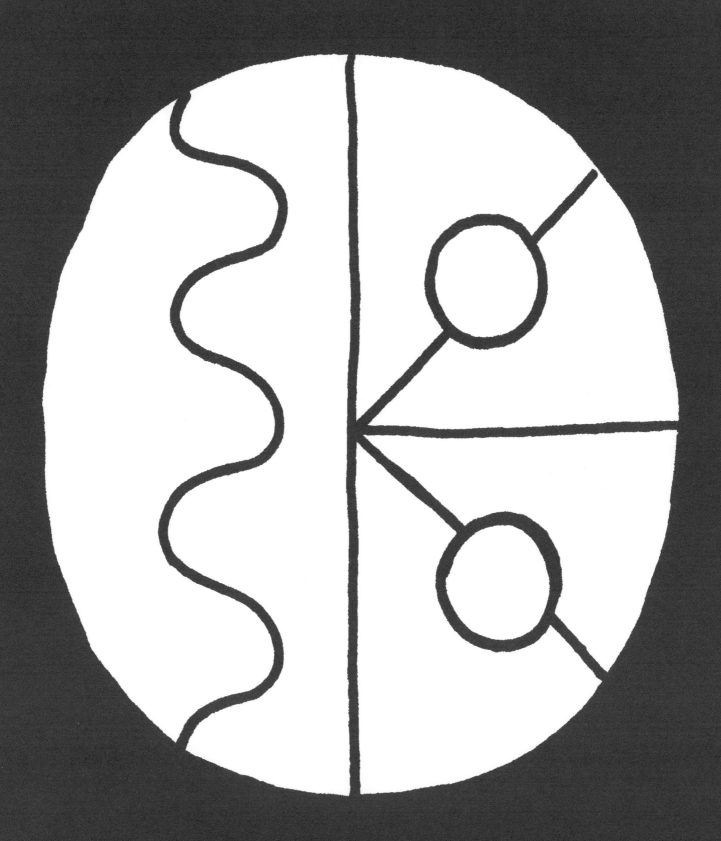

Draw streets running through this town. Add more buildings, vehicles, people, and creatures. What else is in your special town?

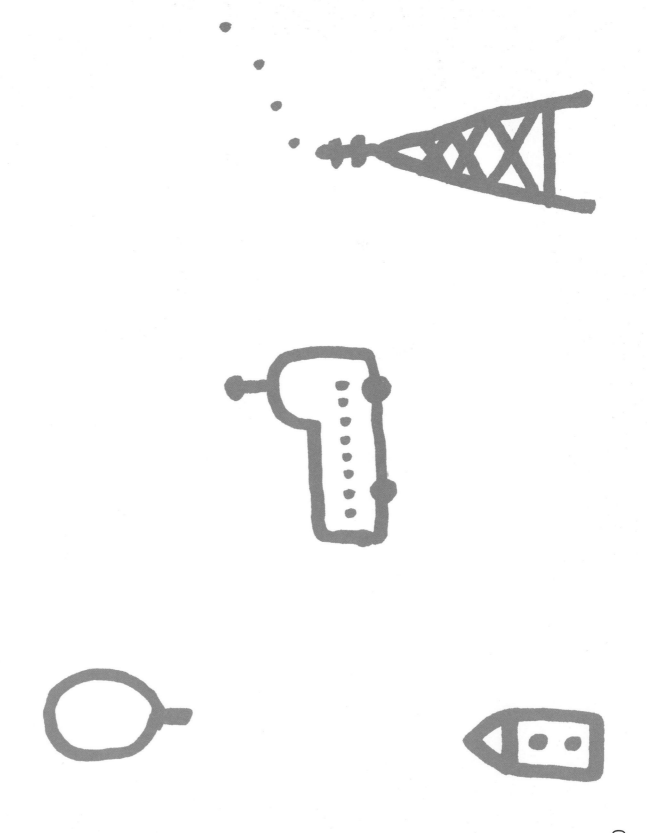

Can you find one tiny tiny fish swimming among the whales?

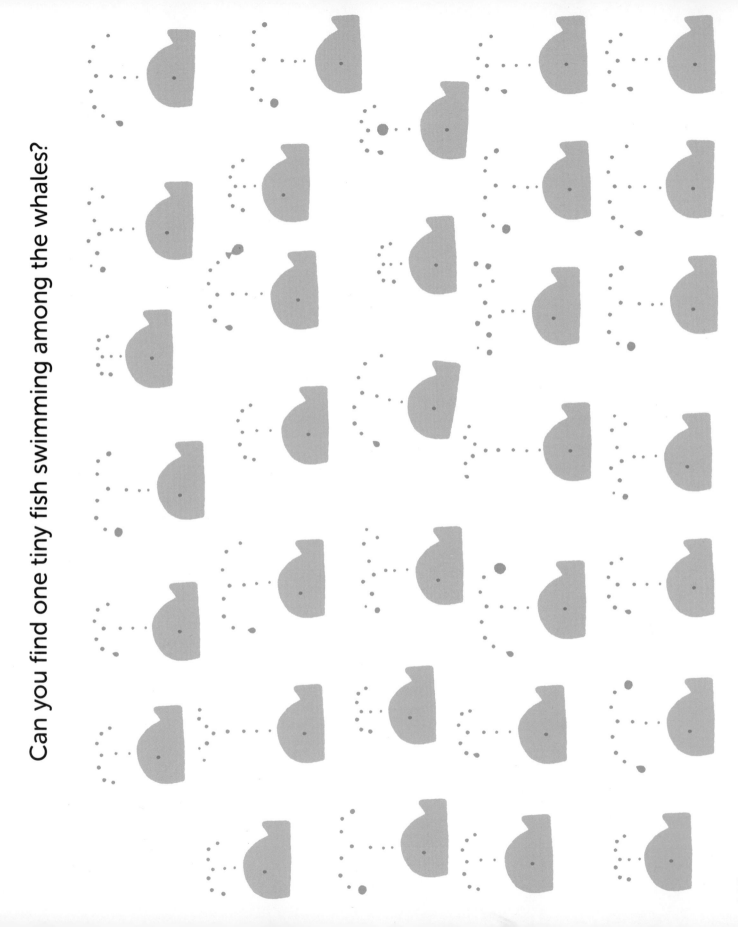